What Follows

T0164165

What Follows

H.R. Webster

www.blacklawrence.com

Executive Editor: Diane Goettel
Cover Design: Crisis
Book Design: Amy Freels

Published 2022 by Black Lawrence Press.
Printed in the United States.

Inside of that world
someone painting
animal-sounds

Inside the dark
huge sounds

—Jean Valentine

Contents

What Follows

Every house I've ever lived in was filled with snakes.
The black snake in the attic, wrist-thick as a man.
The copperhead beneath the couch cushion. Garters'
quick green caulking between the kitchen tiles.
The single timber rattler, invisible except for the tender
husks it left for me, crinoline rustle like a party
dress pulled down over the shoulders then breasts
in a rush. Wherever I went they followed, dragging
their delicate purses of venom, their noise of forage
in the china after dark.

                             The snakes I live with now leave
quieter marks. Long, dark hairs caught between
the paint and the bathroom wall. The animal
musk of water from the tap. The nightmare impression
of a single sharp red nail drawing a part in my hair.
The fear that no matter how many years have passed
any child I bear will be yours. No, will be you.
A little boy, blond and fat, who will industriously beat
at the tall grasses with a stick, will wade into Lake Michigan,
not to swim but to punch the waves with your tiny fists.

Farm & Field

I could talk about the Virginia Creeper turning on the split rail forever.

Cosmos petaling themselves monstrous through the too-long fall.

I'm still wearing the ring that turned my finger green.

Someone has stapled a single panel of clouds over the stirrupped bed in one room

of the clinic. Cherry blossoms in another.

I'm still pulling suckers off the nightshades. Pruning back blossom

end rot even though I'm expecting a frost.

Someone has told my body to telescope towards the kind of pain

we have agreed to call *a pinch*.

I am not sorry for what got me here.

I felt like I had 10,000 tits.

I felt like I had 10,000 tits and they were all being licked at once.

I was the lodestone sewn into the bird.

I was the secondhand trembling in place.

The calendar pages ripping off, the barn-roof tarp, the flock.

It is better, maybe, to talk about horses. Horses ripping up grass.

Let me tell you what I love.

The way they will eat from your hand even when locked in a brimming pasture.

Even when locked in a pasture sugared in rain.

Autocomplete

I can't stop watching teenage boys eat shit at the skatepark.
It gives me real pleasure.

I imagine pulling the stitched pennies of scabs
from their shoulders and knees. A man

barks at me like a dog from the window of his car.
A man shouts *I want to fuck you in the*—

I lost the last word to the parking
lot's rattling sea. I think it was *ass*.

It could have been *mouth*.
The computer can't stop suggesting *yours*—

truly. There are only so many words.
I can't stop reading

articles about the woman who pushed her dead
toddler on a swing for a full night and day.

My mother wouldn't have.
Wouldn't have pushed me I mean.

So few of us are original in our disorder.
The computer can't stop suggesting I begin

To Whom It May Concern. Suggests I might be hurting
my eyes, staring at a screen so long.

It might have been *pussy*, but that seems unlikely.
I imagine pulling the boys' torn

white t-shirts over their heads. They aren't hurt, not really.
Not badly. They don't smell good, that's ok. I run them

hot water. I test it with my wrist—fingers too practiced
to let me know when things are too much.

The computer can't stop suggesting I sell someone
my eggs. *Girls like you can make big money.*

It knows my height because I bought those jeans,
the chimney fire of my marriage,

my student loan debt, breast size.
It must know I am not well, inside, that I have

spent hours reading about the woman
who drove the wrong way down the Taconic Parkway

with a car full of kids. The abscess
of her mouth, the gut's thrum of clear liquor.

People get pissed when they talk about Diane.
I lick every word clean. Still the computer

wants my eggs, the ugly teeming of my
innards. A man sends me a message online:

*I want to cum on your
face/tits/ass.* Strangers know something

the computer doesn't, should have guessed.
There are only so many kinds of girl I am

permitted to be. It is hard not to imagine
a child slinkying down my steep wooden stairs.

The way each thump of the body downward
is inevitable, but still makes my face break

just slightly, the smoke sucked
back into the red hole of my mouth.

I will be at the bottom. I will be watching.
Watching is what I know how to do.

Failure

On his way out he tells me his childhood dog hung herself
on the cord holding open the blinds when left alone a few hours.

It clearly took her some time to die.
Blood on the sofa back. I have thrown away all my books

with phrases like *the willowy willow branches,*
hot August heat. I have made fun of the way language

is always finding its own end. My neighbor's Chihuahua, Lucky Boy,
spinning in circles this morning when I bend to touch his face.

He survived 30 days alone in coyote country before someone found him
who wanted him. I have made fun of these failures but here I am saying

this sadness is sad. I am always buying those little bottles of milk
that indicate loneliness. He will come over again tomorrow to jack off

pressed against me. He will leave and I will lie down
in the easy blue of television and beer. The wallow and blank

like the thick bank of tulips between East and West
bound highways. I like home improvement shows, couples

smashing the bedroom wall, ripping down velvet valances, pressing their palms
to the cool cheek of a new marble countertop. My dog would be certain to eat

my face if I died and didn't feed him dinner. My milk has already begun to clot.

Scaphism

Yesterday two men told me my skin smells like good milk and grass.
Hay put away wet will burst into flames.

I slept with them both. After, one added—*and butter too.*
His hands shook before the evening's first beer—a flank under flies.

Horses put away wet will tie-up, colic on cold water.
One in the morning. One in the night. I showered in between.

The ancient Persians would feed liars milk and honey,
smear their face hands and feet, and lay them between two boats,

one smaller than the other. The places on my body they press their faces to:
anything scooped out. Set on a stagnant lake, it took days to die.

Days for the boats to fill with shit and wasps.
The milky skin to be stung away.

I am both ashamed and not ashamed.
I like to tell the truth. I like to make men love me

with my body. But I am always afraid. Afraid
and leaden with power. Here, the barn

is wet and burning. The horses sick and they can't spit it out.

Ritual

He says he thinks I want to see his cock.
He says *I promise it won't hurt you.*
Outside, a car crash claps. It's 4 o'clock,
the cat has peed behind the fridge, and through
the pane the streets unleash the day's long heat,
the ants draw dark cartography around
a squirrel, her red insides. The curtains beat
against the reeling fan. All over town
young boys walk home with clarinets, the bus
sighs and brakes; it kneels like a girl. The bricks
loose as children's teeth. The chickadees fuss
over bread mixed with earth. He lifts his dick
like a candle, a bird. It does not light
the growing dark, does not lift its wings in flight.

Tender

In zombie movies there's always a couple who fuck
one last time, drink some wine & just give up.

This is the only reason I can think of to fall in love again.
On first dates men often ask *how would you rather die,*

I kid you not, *drowning or fire.* They want to know my body even as it's destroyed
by my imagination. It's the end of the world & we can't stop saying the word *tender.*

It's the only language left for flesh, for helplessness, the desire to be kind, etc.
It's the secret name of every shirtless photo sent me

from the gym bathroom, clattering with light. The sloppy calligraphy
of the ten-point buck half-velveted & hoisted for the camera

on their dating profiles. Strop of tongue. I want to be touched like the belly wants meat
or pills, some new combination of words. On first dates I always make sure to say

I have a lazy left eye. After, they rub their thumbs against my thigh—
a scratch-off ticket. They want to know my body as it loosens its leash. Baby teeth

unhooked in their holsters. Slack bight of muscle in the face, pendant chain
still tangled in my hair when I turn on the bathroom light. In movies

there's always one gutsy little zombie dragging herself forward
by the elbows, as if I would do anything undead but lie in bed

watching reality dating shows and gnawing off my own hand.
In this episode the man is eating great platters of cold cuts,

in this one the women are crying in the badlands, their hair-dos ruined
& revealing scalp. They have the hacksaw voices of sorority sisters

& flames taking a house to the studs. There's a virgin there's a widow a zombie
in paste jewelry shoving rose petals in her jaw. They keep rasping

tender tender tender but it's been dubbed
into a series of questions and answers about what they fear most.

Close-Up Magic

After Jose Ahonen's Youtube Video "Taikuutta koirille – Magic for Dogs"

The magician's hand
is a mouth swallowing
into his wrist. Flaw in the palm's
horizon. Disappearances rust
industriously inside us.
Busy flecks of pain.
Dogs shown close-up magic
kiss the palm's empty salt lick.
Again and again. The way girls
on reality TV whisper *thank you*
into the ear of the man tasked
with their dismissal. The crinkle
of their bare spines in backless
dresses, the thin lines earrings
have stretched into their lobes.

+

You know what it is to be composed
of absence. To spell out
your existence only with the lamp
which won't turn off despite
the flicking of the switch,
the rocking chair, the oily
handprint on the glass. To name
yourself by the carton
of double-yolked eggs, the typo
in the text, the echo of the motion
sensor light between snow and snow
heavy sky, underneath the heavy
pelt of pines.

Snapdragon

At night the ghost lays my body out
on the sticky counterpane.

Like solitaire, like carnations.
My skin the safety glass

graffitied with a pin. My hair
the rope hung over

the river from a dead limb.
My face lifts a wing to preen, to bite

its feathers smooth. Outside the window
the gap-toothed night is all lattice,

all cantilever, all boxwoods musking
up the dark. The wind

is the perpetual motion of a fist
opening inside me—a game

revealing a blue packet
of sweetener, an empty palm.

My hands are leaves, limp
with drought, a little girl's

thin plaits. The strings I use
to lift them by the wrists

have been cut, retied
by someone else. The ghost

covers my mouth with its hand:
all dial soap, all silhouettes, all calluses

from plucking chords. Now
that my mouth is covered it occurs

to me that I should scream.
Because I love the ghost,

because I have been raised
to do what I am told,

I open my mouth.
The ghost waits,

a rusted bolt,
for tonight's syrup-dose

of sound. But I scream silent
as snapdragons, dried

on their stalk, skulls
ruffled at the sockets

and mouth like the hem
of that sweet summer dress,

with its thin shoulder straps, three
cloth-covered buttons at the chest.

Inheritance

I wait for her in the municipal park
all morning. I wear the paper dress.
My hands are buried in the sandbox.
The swing set swings
its stirrups white with bird shit.

She comes, her arms pulled
inside her t-shirt. She comes,
her silver instrument
already measuring.

She ties off my wrist with wire,
with the ribbed plastic
ribbon of a balloon, twine
that held in a chicken's neck
and gizzards, hair from her thick
red braid, string pull
of the naked bulb.

The hand grows white.

+

She enters without knocking
to search my bureau for a forgotten
garment. Covers one breast
with her hand. Bees pour out the other.

Her voice is a fruit basket
full of bites. My trellis rots
inside the bloom of her breath
on the plate glass. She snaps
the auditorium silent as a bruise,

lifts herself over the threshold
on her many elbows, forgets to mail
the dripping envelope.

Holds a pendant chain
in her mouth
like a bit.

+

I am sitting at the kitchen
table. She is cutting vegetables
and humming to herself. I open
my lips to tell her I love her
but my mouth
is filled with bulbs
and she is already walking me
towards the garden.

Rabbit Test

My father calls to tell me about the cat
he rolled over in his sleep.

The chill of her body in bed
when he woke.

Do I owe him the rabbit now?
Do I owe her drowning—

her piss-soaked purse her satin
lining, owe the slam

of her body against the wall.
        Mercy me.

I'll keep it tucked in by the sly rot
of my back teeth

next to the bitter herb
its coat of blood the feminine

ruffle of its leaves
when I drew it from me.

Folk cure for future, cinnamon
and rue. Doubled doubled, a perpetual

vibration like a knife
in a target, silhouette

of a buck. Won't tell him I could not
peel her cleanly of her skin.

I think of the rabbit when I open
the leatherette album,

spread it over the white wall-to-wall:
my father's eyes shut when he tips

the cup to his lips. The wolf spider
catching light. The waterfall's zipper

split with his narrow shoulders,
the broken neon sign: MO EL,

the kitten rubbing his cheek
on the day lilies by the door.

The earliest snapshot:
my father's infant face,

the mask he wore bitten
from a slice of bread.

Persona

Hello I am the dead black cat on the curb across the street from your best friend's house.

Hello I am the dead tooth at the front of his mouth.

Hello I am the black cat, not dead, but in the posture of death, on the porch of the house when he comes out to greet you.

Hello I am my knuckles, jeweled with ant poison.

Hello I am the Hardees 2-piece combo I ate in secret. Ate to punish you for driving us home drunk.

Hello I am the rust-gut corolla on the shoulder of the highway, white take-out bag lung from the cracked window.

Hello I am the plastic bag, surrendering.

Hello I am the frightening inches of spice smell under oaks.

Hello I am the knife's simple mechanism.

Hello, it me.

What you say when you wake me up—beer-drunk and dog-bit. *It me.* When you meet me at the commuter rail station. When you tap your fingers against the frosted shower stall to let me know you are out there, pissing. When I say *it me* I mean *it me* with your voice in my mouth. What love feels like today.

It me, sitting in the car, waiting for you and wondering how I know

which cat is living and which dead.

Despite no evidence of motion, no heave.

Dog Bite

At the end of this poem the dog dies.
8 months later, the winter you got sober, after the third attack.
We are most dangerous when we are ashamed. I tried

To forgive him, picked blue plums from the tree where he was chained, still alive
But alone nights in the orchard, baying at the coyotes' musky tracks.
At the end of this poem the dog dies.

In August I straddled your chest, cut out the black stitches under your eye
With sewing scissors, the crane's bladed beak. *Is he still handsome?* my mother asks.
We are most dangerous when we are ashamed. I tried

To picture your face, the moment before you called the dog to you, but after your lie:
Just 3 drinks, your mouth a dripping rip. I was afraid before the blood, knew already,
    perhaps,
That at the end of this poem the dog dies.

But that night, bruising under waiting room fluorescents, we begged for his life, falsified
Our story to the hospital cops. They snapped their gum, boots pants pen gun, all black.
We are most dangerous when we are ashamed. I try

To turn away. Your cheek enters his rough mouth. Did he know a danger I could not yet
    identify?
A forbidden thought. But remember, love, that summer's bared, thirsty syntax?
We are most dangerous when we are ashamed. I tried.
At the end of this poem the dog dies.

Stench

When you want to die I want to die. Open the door on the freeway, unbuckle, & tip.
Safety razor smashed open with the heavy bottom of the jam jar head

into sheetrock into the corner of the coffee table from kneeling.
I'm not proud of it. Cheap curtain soaking in fry oil. You passed through

the lobby on your way to the elevator. A vase of lilies,
rotting on the console. I could smell them on you

when you got home, funereal. Could smell the panic attack
20 minutes out, snow on mittens boxed up until fall, trashfires

when you are homesick, garlic three days later the scent
in the gusset of my panties. You can't have secrets & I'm sorry.

The weekend my grandfather died you got high
two days straight. I knew at the airport at the curb on your wool coat

Could have smelled your collar smelled all the men on the stoop
fingered who you bought from. Like the dogs your brother trains

in prison who sniff your breath then dial 911 with their velveted noses.
Their velcro harnesses *don't pet me I'm working.*

Thick loop of leash. I'm holding an egg yolk in my mouth
you spit it there I woke up like this. Woke syrup, rhythmed, sick.

Leap from the fire escape gun in my palm
even though we don't own a gun I can't lift my hand.

I'm wearing some invisible ponderous bracelet.
Even from the other room. Pause the TV shout

are you thinking about dying. Sometimes you say *yes*
sometimes *no* but confess later, *yes.* 9mm in my palm even though

I don't know what that means had to look it up. Once I was date raped
by a man wearing cologne. Salt, cedar, lead. Drove myself home. Lay myself down

on my bed could smell it on the cat for weeks after. The way he hung
his pants carefully over the back of the chair. I know when it is your desire

not mine because I would take pills & you want to die the way boys want to die.
Overpass ceiling fan walk into the sea. Can't hold a penny in my palm

without the toothache of copper odor know what ants taste like
& the grain you feed horses though I've never put them in my mouth.

Horses, I dreamed of them & I smelled them in the morning.
Horses, you dreamed of them I smelled them in the morning.

Remember lilies say lilies smell lilies on your neck.
Think of death, smell lilies smell your neck. No, God, I am the smell

of lilies now, what horror is this. I am the sickening lilies dropping
pistils on the tablecloth staining it with pollen staining it, stained by it.

Hellraiser

I wanted the way the back of the hand
wanted the nail, once. The sprawling fist
of black crickets the mouth. The throat two pins
to curtain her open to coarse whisper.
You called me a bitch, the third time, last night.
I can say *I love you* but cannot show you
my breasts, anymore, or let you strike me,
there, and on my face, during sex. I bend
my body away, dressing, twist the bra
around, and flip the cups up over me
like the eyes closing on a body hung
by the ankles. I want to want skinless-
ness, fingers in mouth/soft neck be rats
nailed to the wall, my teeth to click and click.

His Master's Voice

You walk the dog the long way
round the transit center now.
Yesterday he licked up a sluice of vomit

pink with wine when you turned your head.
Your long index finger stroking for a chicken bone
stuck in his ridged black throat last week.

He lunges for the dropped ice cream cone,
the slice of cherry cake in cellophane hungered after
then forgotten on the curb.

The long way now, past the bar
with its bubbling neon coupe of beer
where you stopped in secret

for months, then rinsed your mouth, spat,
came home. I like the scene in movies where a letter is read
in the voice of the writer, dead or absent.

The narration lets us know the woman standing
alone in the kitchen with the page in her hand
has the man's voice in her head. That voice and word

cannot be snapped apart, the slip of meat
between ulna and radius the dog wants most.
Rather, I like that it is impossible

for a movie to show the woman and the letter any other way.
The sea was once a gasping mouth of wine-stained teeth
and tongue because there was no blue.

Once, the world pressed flat against the wall,
the saints' noses resting on their cheeks,
shoulders as close as the sky, the broken plates of their halos.

There's a solitary bite taken from the pepperoni slice
dropped on the curb by Red, who loves to kiss the dog
on the mouth, talk to the dead, drink Steel Reserve,

spit into a plastic cup. I ask the dog questions in my voice
and answer them in the voice of the dog. I want to know
if he remembers anything from before he was born, his dreams,

if he has another name for himself. I want to know
if everyone looked at the saints
and said *this is not what the world should look like*

but I don't know how to fix it. The dog doesn't
remember anything but sit, lie down, the sound of your tread
on the stairs at night. He rings the bell

looped over the knob because he wants to go outside.
I hear this whole poem in your voice although
I am the writer and the woman standing

in the kitchen, page folded into thirds.
You leave the house without saying goodbye.
I love you and I want you to be alive

today and the next day too.
The ringing bell, the dog choking
on his treat. *Ring-ring,* your voice.

Your voice, the silence of the bone.

Hapax Legomenon

When I wake to piss he sleep-talks to me.
His voice like foreign coins glued to the floor,
Water slopping on slanted glass. A key
snapped in the lock. Landscapes, and landscapes more.
I decided to be a happy girl,
and I was. The conventional lyric:
salt, pony, vena cava. Hollowed burl
of belly cataloging generic
abandon. My mouth wet with permission.
Decided to thumb off my plum's wax bloom.
Can I say etcetera yet? Use diction
as plain as his, asleep in our room:
Slut. His dreaming mouth is so precise.
I get up, go pee, lie down, close my eyes.

Isabella Stewart Gardner

I've read witnesses to medieval torture were jealous
of those broken on the wheel. Their sainted flesh made tentacle.

All else dims before agony.

> Smell of the sponge on the bottom of the cup.
> Balding crown.
> Carsickness.
> Splinter, niggling in heel.

There is a rabbit and then there is the letter
hidden inside the rabbit. The mouth
of St. Michael's beast and his belly-mouth too. I once thought my worst

instinct the reliquary: A cigarette from Brahms's saucer licked
into an envelope. A scrap of white silk a fringed glove a fingernail.

A man's grieving face when I'm on top.
My waist-length braid secreted in my mother's bottom drawer.
> Tea-stained egg,
> shank, gem of blood baked into dough,
> thimble of salt water.

I was mistaken in this belief.

In the walled garden you fit your fingertips with nasturtiums,
their furred neck holes. Infant Christ's withered little brows,

his hands squeezing a flat
note from a trapped bird. In Belorussian folklore,
you tell me, ferns flower once a year, at night.

Ferns you hunted as a child, luck-crazed, eyelashed.
While you're in the gift shop B. says, *I like him,*
but I need to break up with him.
                              He wants to kiss my feet.

I often wonder if I possess desires I have failed to imagine.
The dimples of spores on undersides. The shallow forest,
the swallowed ring, the glowing

lamp of skin.   *Hurt me, Daddy, please.*
Outside Minsk the cabbage fields
refuse to grow. Or people refuse to eat from them,

I often have my stories/fingers crossed.   Myth fistful

of my mouth. You left because you knew you could be beaten for loving

what you loved—the photograph you snapped this morning before the bus
to the museum: B. naked in the skim light, his neck tipped back, tap water

from a wine glass. You left the fields rimming the city, fallow
with ash-fed ferns hay scent and sexed

by wind, where my great grandparents were shot
(without flourish) in the head and back.
                    Oh, B.'s lovely feet, the coarse black epaulet of hair.

Weather

The radiator rattles like a ghost at the banister.
I have forgotten, again, the bread.

When you look away I shake salt into my palm. Lick it clean.
There are two light switches in the kitchen.

Some days the switch on the right turns on the light. Some days the left. Some
small disorders are pacts of estrangement:

the crooked venetian blind, the wilting and half-remembered hum of the pop
song passed back and forth. Low, venereal.

We have nothing to talk about but the weather. We have nothing
to talk about but how the weather used to be.

October, and the plows already kiss the road to sullen sparks.
The tulip poplars break the electricity's humming thread.

We goblin ourselves with flashlights. We fill the bathtub
with water. We eat the meat. We drink the milk the cream.

The refrigerator warm with the canine smell
of butter. Mold rapidly fingering up edges.

The snowy lawn broken by desire lines in the dark.
In a week the grass revealed. In a week the mail

still missing, the men with chainsaws not yet come to cut
the broken branches from the ruined rows of trees.

A week and we still can't speak, don't have anything
to speak of but snow and Octobers

in the happy loneliness of childhood, buried to the neck in brittle leaves.

Love Language

I want this poem to end on the line: the dullest knife is the most dangerous.
I want to talk about the cherry candy ball gag you bought me.

The time I got my period at the casino and fucked up
the smoke-wet coverlet. The knife is in the poem because you were pissed

I took the job at the factory. The knife and the board and the wet rag
holding the board tight to the stainless-steel table. A pallet of cabbages, baby

heads and basketballs. You wanted to knock me up. You wanted to pay my rent.
I still have airline credit in your name. You bought me paper bags of mini-bar bottles,

gift certificates to stores only teenagers shop at. I've had a romper and a sheer top
in my shopping cart for weeks now. A bra with daisies over the nipples. I smelled

like cardboard all the time. Produce too long in the walk-in. Inside my head
was a funnel cupping a funnel cupping another on the wire rack. Pollen

on the folding chair in the smoking area. A killdeer faking it in the parking lot.
At the casino I had pneumonia. Pneumonia is almost a flower, I guess.

Though that's a stretch. I told you not to buy them for me and you didn't.
You did buy me an eye exam though because I squinted all the time.

Sudafed and a couple hundred to lose at blackjack. I wonder when they have time
to vacuum the acres of flame-print carpet. 24 hours of Pretty Kitty slot machines

and someone always playing. I ate shrimp cocktail and drank vodka martinis,
paper cones of free root beer. I puked in the rain shower. I ended it eventually

but I can't say why. My hair was dropping out in a drench
my wrists covered in salt rash. Didn't like thinking about where we both were in 1999.

I'm an old soul though, I'm told. And my knees hurt and my skin is starting to give
like grapes too long in the crisper. Your list of what's disgusting: pubic hair beyond

the crease of the thigh, that she didn't list your name on the acknowledgements page.
My manager says *she has good energy* whenever the new girl has pretty hair

caught up in the corona of her blue sanitary net. You called every woman
your age crazy, wore more cologne kissed with more tongue had more secret

rage than boys my age. A few weeks after I ended it you invited yourself over. Crushed
on my loveseat you cupped my jaw turned my face to yours squeezed

my mouth open. I was a little drunk. I ate a slice of bread I wanted to sober up.
I was afraid. I'm pretty fuzzy on most of the times I've been raped

and wanted to remember this. But you left. I'm not accusing you of anything.
I've never told anyone you fucked me. Although grabbing my arm

at the holiday party was a bad idea. I was a little drunk shoving bread into my mouth
but you had your fingers in there also. Mostly you wanted to make me cry,

which I get. Wanted me to know I hurt a lot of people, and you never
really liked my dog. *You don't even have a love language*

you said. That's not the first time someone has told me something like that,
but it's the stupidest way to say it I've ever heard. My favorite factory task

was folding boxes. Then running the label machine. I like things where you can get
a sick rhythm going. I hated working the Hobart, the handle left blisters in the "L"

of my thumb. I never cut myself once and was proud of how fast my hands went.
The way I could make shortcuts in the margins of a shift. They don't belong in a poem,

those efficient little gestures, the left hand ready for what the right hand wrought,
the same songs on the radio every day, the line humming like a weapon.

That pissed you off, I think. That I like doing even the stupidest jobs well.
Chopping cabbage at twice the rate of the frat boy across the table.

And work took up my afternoons. I couldn't keep coming over to drink and rough up
my face against your shaved chest while your kids were at school.

After that night you started dating a girl my age in public. Everyone saw you kiss her.
If that's what you call love language then you can fuck right off.

I bet you are wondering how I'm going to get back to the knife if I never cut myself.
Wondering if I cut you and you just didn't notice before now. A vent forming

on your smooth palm as you read, the first split second of a molt, a cocoon
slitting open. I think that was a joke about your age. But that would make me

a dulled blade. I hate myself, but not that much. Everyone I know is getting married
and they all want a poem for the ceremony. I recommend Billy Collins, the knife

and the bread, etc. Everyone listens even though I hate Billy Collins I'm divorced
and I say the word dick a lot. Even though I somehow ended up on a night shift

with you despite the factory job I started every morning at 7. You never asked
whether I wanted the money. Took the condom off the first night we fucked.

What do you call work you don't decide to do? Work that is done to you?
I know lots of girls who choose to suck dick & cam for a living and it seems as good

or bad as any job. But that wasn't what I intended, I just touched your arm
and laughed one too many times and ended up at the casino,

saying thank you until I puked. I guess I would prefer total freedom, but for now
I like doing even the smallest jobs with grace. I'm a good line cook, can fold hospital

corners into a sheet and clean a hotel toilet so well you forget what was done to it before
you arrived. It was really easy to make you cum with my mouth.

It was really easy to say that I loved you. Maybe I won't ever get back
to the knife. Maybe the knife is this poem. There's a few people out there

who know your name, would be pissed about you breaking the bed
with me tied to it, twisting my back like ribbed balloon ribbon on a branch.

Maybe the knife is my love language. I've never done the quiz. Maybe the knife
is just the knife, and I'm at my place on the line, the fatigue mats overlapped

so I trip each time I shift my weight to keep my blood pressure from dropping.
The manager slipping up behind me with the whetting stone. Step off

he says, and run the sanitizer for 20. You're a liability with that blade.
Don't you know the dullest knife is the most dangerous. But here you are, ruining

my ending. Showing up at my house unannounced with an eighth of weed, a ball
gag, and a bag of limes. Baby gets what baby wants. I say thank you I say

thank you I say thank you I say thank you I say thank you I say nothing
because your hands are in my mouth again.

Voicemails

You call and say *I know you misbehaved*.
I am in bed with him, the dog chewing
a hole in your grey sweater, my back caved
in, its pale taut thread—snapped. He's undoing
my breath, ripping out my seams. Ravel, rend.
In a South Jersey ward my grandma bites
through the tip of her finger. She pretends
to recall my recorded voice, rewrites
our love song: you a soldier, me a nurse.
Her brain's slow tangle of blood, dark hair left
on the pillow. I drown your lack in verse,
in cock, you call five times while I'm possessed.
She thinks you send me letters from the front,
your only epistle this voicemail: *you cunt*.

Occlusion

Some flaws in gemstones are invisible
except the shadows they throw inside.
From the Latin for *shut up*. A feasible
metaphor for most anything. You cried
while you told me a stranger whispered *sex*
in your ear at the Stop & Shop, again
when you were walking your dog down the steps
from the street to the sea. Look at the stain
in the diamond. It's not the thing itself,
but what's left of the light that was swallowed.
That's your analogy, here's mine as well:
It's exhausting, this fear of being followed.
That's not a metaphor. I'm not a man.
I have no pretty ways to say it left.

+ +

What Follows

For Marmie and Oma

> *ruin arrives*
> *ruin does not leave*
> *it comes tolling over the generations*
> *it comes rolling the black night salt up from the ocean floor*
> *and all your thrashed coasts groan*
>
> *—Anne Carson,* Antigonick

During the play the audience laughs when the mother stabs herself in the liver. Surprised at the revelation of innards, of a body more than loose sack of blood, breasts.

+

Sorting through your books deciding what to throw away I flip the page to the Great War. Stop stacking. Strange today that all the men are suddenly singular to me. Disentangled from the mass of history. Something breaks. Something breaks, inside. The books are thick, rough-edged pages meant to appear freshly cut.

+

Death came and took from you a virginity you did not know you possessed, but guarded, closely.

+

My crying has become so constant, I could set a clock by it. But these days I can't wash time off my hands. It is everywhere. What comes from my mouth is useful only if you have use for noise. Like the noise of the sea, so familiar you have renamed it silence. Like the noise of the sea, a lead blanket that keeps the body dark.

+

At Gallipoli one soldier recorded that he wept at night, not because he feared death, but because he was so dirty. He lay awake in the furrow of limbs. The flies so much like air they entered the body, its nine holes, at all hours.

+

I wear two left shoes into the church. I let my cousin's baby yank the silver chain that threads your ring around my neck. I let his spit stain remain on my chest. I read a poem to the congregation. A bad poem. It has the word angels in it. It has the word angles in it. Words become a dirty white thread tangled in the zipper of my throat.

+

During the plane ride home someone begins to pray loudly. Later, in the airport bathroom a woman in the next stall drops her bloody tampon on the floor. She begins to cry. I leave without washing my hands. The paper towel dispensers unscroll their clean blank tongues as I walk by. I don't want to see her face.

+

Even though you have been cremated, your tidy white cardboard box tucked in the earth, I'm still busying my hands with the dirt of your body in death. The laundry you left in the machine, the mold tenderly threading through your underthings. And then the mold on the bread in the refrigerator, ticking off the hours crumb by crumb.

+

In Germany they call the First Battle of Ypres *The Massacre of the Innocents*. They were singing as they died. Wearing flower crowns like brides before blood stains the bed. Like brides desperate to see the seashore. To be washed rough by saltwind. To smell vetiver over the hot thickness of gunscent and horse belly turned inside out.

+

During the play the audience coughs in long columns of noise. The fall sickness snaps a clean sheet over the little theater, the couples in their best shoes. You hid your jewelry in a paper box, in the pocket of a spare bathrobe hung on the back of a door. Their bodies hide diseases, little jewels of coming pain. A ring with three stones, a thinly tangled golden chain.

+

I fill out the family history forms. Cancer. Cancer. Cancer. The heel of my hand spreads the cheap ink. Letters drawing back like hair in the wind. I want to lie, to say I am a good enough girl not to get sick like the others. I want to know the truth, have them cut away everything.

+

At Passchendaele boys drowned in the mud. You in your lungs. We don't talk here about how our women die. What fruit rots first. We are left with no way to predict our own ruins. Blank boxes on medical questionnaires, white crosses marching namelessly across the broken landscape when the fighting finally passed. No words to tell the doctors, tap this organ first. It's the breasts, no, something else.

+

Nights in the narrow stall of your shower I check my body over. As though I have been walking in the forest. I have been walking in the forest and am feeling for the blood swollen insects. The ticks at my nape, in the crease beneath my rump. Hoping for a strangeness that the fingers can find and name. I feel for it even inside my mouth, between the tender vaults of its ceiling.

+

Death makes us behave like strangers. I go to Delaware, play catch with my little cousins. This is the only way not to be small inside the body's auditorium, its echoes. To throw things, badly. To run in the shorn grass along the river. Shout *I got it I got it.* Let the ball drop just short of my open palms. The dog rests its paws on my funeral skirt, presses muzzle to belly. People who say black doesn't show dirt have it all wrong. From the park I send strangers messages from my phone: *Lie on top of me & lie on top of me & lie on top of me.*

+

During the play the dirt of death is given to the woman. She takes it in her cupped palms. She raises it to her lips, like water. Like she is speaking to it in tones too quiet for the audience to hear.

Beta Vulgaris

Let's make sugar, my father said. We began
with the garden's blank grid, measured out
rows with tape and rod, the taut demand

of thread, of wire. We tuned the flat earth
behind the old machine shed, turned
the key toward sweetness, each fourth

row planted marigolds whose bitter punch
of scent and sun set the mule deer's velvet
noses towards other gardens, toward the plunge

of burning irrigation ditches and coyotes
rubbing the night all wrong, while the beets
tightened their fists around the earth's dark throat.

+

Drought stepped ponderous over our sky, dragged
its shimmering bad leg behind. Heat made black snakes
on the road where there were none. Wet rags

around our throats, we knelt to pull two plants of three
from every row, to pinch their green candles out.
Evenings the eastern sky would bruise and preen

with heat lightning, nothing more. Thirsty,
beets lose sweetness fast, grow bitter
around their lack. We went to bed still dirty,

saved our slim allotment of water for the plants.
My father snapped like my finger in the slamming door.
He ground clots of dirt to dust between his furious hands.

+

Fresh fire in the foothills
and something wrong in the soil. Gravel
marked our knees when we knelt to weed. I willed

the leaves to grow past the width of my now-crooked finger.
We pulled purslane, red threaded
as an eyelid, thistles that dried to thick tinder

for the prairie to flint. When finally we began to rip
the beets up by their leaves, the roots were smaller
than we had hoped. We dumped their foliage, its broken ribs,

in the pasture to steam and rot,
gathered their dirty knuckles in buckets,
left our spades to rust in the gutted plot.

+

All day we sliced them thin
into the heavy-bottomed pot. We added sugar, hoped
the liquid would gather at its geometry. Hoped its rim

of sweetness was enough for the beets to cling
against. Sugar begets sugar, we prayed. Then watched
as my father failed to wring

some goodness from the dirt.
The crystals that formed were too few to fill
his callused palm. We ate them for dessert;

their penny taste stayed on our tongues
for all the years we lived with my father
by the garden. All the years that we were young.

+

Late that night I walked the pulp
out to the edge of the prairie, past the quiver
of miller moths who lingered by the motion-sensor light's dim bulb.

I left the mush in the prairie's gloom
for the mountain lions who waited in the cottonwoods,
or for the small creatures those lions would come to consume.

Spring

The rain rubs against the rain
like a boy in the night.

The body does not
fit into itself.

The rain is not blameless.
It has drowned

the plums and made
the chickens hungry for flesh.

They are hushed in the wet
ragweed. Stirring only to tear apart

a mouse thrown
into their midst. It runs

without eyes, ears, tail,
legs. A blur of blood.

Then stillness. Next the birds
will begin to eat the eggs.

My Mother Says "I'm Going to Flush the Toilet Now"

at the end of our call. She wants me to know she wasn't peeing
while we spoke, just hiding in the bathroom
so my father would not know we were on the phone.

This morning she helped the young men from down the road
unload the hay into the close darkness of the hayloft. The wet spring means she needs
extra bales to tide the herd over. She calls them "the girls"—the animals

she loves and names and will kill to eat. The air in the barn is thick and moted.
The cobwebs garland light when the door swings wide. She forgot to wear her mask,
to keep her busted lungs from the boys' wet breath. My father

is angry. He won't say it and she won't either. Her voice low below
the running tap. He is angry the way I remember. The way he lifted his hand
over her body like a rabbit trap a wire noose sprung back

and hooked to a whipping branch. After she flushes and hangs up I call him, pretend
to hear the story for the first time. He is in the kitchen,
his finger graphing viral death tolls in the air, potatoes foaming over on the stove.

What if fear of punishment is not what makes us good? He wants to know
what precautions I have taken: the blue gloved finger selecting unleaded
at the pump, the empty buses breezing through the 4 way stop, squatting

to piss behind the tractor trailer so I won't enter someone's house.
I don't tell him about the woman punched in the head by cops
the flag we stole and burned the broken cruiser window the tear gas

cough. It's been unseasonably hot, I say. The dog hates the fireworks
and the neighbor's heavy metal through the wall. I'm still sewing masks the rent is due
the bars are open but no, I haven't gone inside. It's hot here too, he tells me, quiet.

Only the crabapples make pink noise in the corners of the mind,
the feeder pigs loose in the yard flop with sunburn, their shorn tails
useless against the hatching flies. My period came early, after we were gassed.

I pulled off the pepper-sprayed mask. I ate hot greasy chicken from the tienda
with my dirty hands, screamed at a helicopter and it screamed back. I say it's hot, yes,
though it threatens rain every afternoon. He thinks my mother needs to be punished

so she will not get sick and die. He will not touch her the rest of the day.
Or touch what she has touched. She is in the garden. The plants are little torches in the
    straw.
Who would I be without punishment? I hear the seedlings blazing, crackling in the
    earth.

I hear her put her naked fingers to the flame.

Late Peaches

At the kitchen sink
I peel the peaches
from their down.
Outside the narrow
window, the marshland billows
with the shy hysteria
of doves, purple phlox
in the rush-shade.

I strip the fruit
the way the man took
the skin from an animal,
the tug and slip
of the knife, fingers hot
under fur. The fox skull
crushed. He's breathless.
Up the elbow, red.

Apiary

For Wang Dalin, who wore 52 pounds of bees

The queen silver
caged around your throat.
You whisper to her
and step onto the scale.
Say: *I am the bride
and you my handmaiden.*
Say: *Bring me my veil.*
Then shake her gently until
she looses perfume.

+

That year the mares were sickly
and the summer squash cracked
hollow under the weight of leaves
and beetle-burrowed blooms. The beebread
rotted in the combs. The swarm gathered
too late in the season. The Beekeeper gave chase.
The boys in the truck bed slapped
their palms on the rusted cab roof.
The swarm swept west
to the hay field.

I was left in the garden,
quivering, my mouth
open, the bees pouring in.

+

In preparation you
must wear shorts that hug the skin.
The bees will enter you.
Must wear goggles over the eyes.
To close them is not enough.

The bees will enter you.
Must wear plugs in nose and ears.
The bees will enter there too.
Must press your lips together.
It is not enough, they want what is within.

+

The Beekeeper taught me
first: do not fear the bees.
Pulled me into the cedars
behind the hive lifted
me and pressed
my ear to the hot tin roof
of the super. Held me there
so I could listen to them move
against each other.
Later I knelt
to gather leaves for smoke.
The drowsing choke of bodies
was the earliest loneliness,
veil still of air.

+

Dearest Bee-Wearer,
is it possible to remain unmoving
under their search and shudder?
To be without breath? Become the
mass of eyes?

They are your breath, be still.
Hold your arms from your
body. Veil yourself in
the dark living heat.

+

The weight tallied,
a white-gloved woman
lifts the silver chain
and withered queen
from within your bee-heavy chest.
They are pulled
from you in handfuls.
This is when the bees
begin to sting.

The Calf

She was born too slow. Hooked hip, hooked breath.
She could stand, could nurse, but could not stand and nurse at once.
The udder's dripping purse just above her reaching lips.

Her mother rubbed the afterbirth off against the shingled door—
streak like a slasher handprint on the near side of the window
to let you know the mask, the tooth, the saw and child were inside all along.

My mother brought the calf to live with us
in the shower stall of the pink-carpeted master bath
where I loved her through the frosted glass.

My hair was a wasp nest then. We had five shoeboxes
filled with dropper-drinking baby squirrels. All my teeth were tied
to slamming doors. She lived a week. Sucked my fingers

to the quick and smelled of sick. Our cemetery was already full
of glass-crazed crows, a raccoon, shot when he wouldn't look away,
the quails we raised from eggs, holding them to the incubator bulb

to see the chick sharpening inside, like muscling a telescope into focus
over a blue-red star. The loose joints of death when we carried her.
The way I pretended to be asleep when we pulled up to the house at night.

Close my eyes and think: look at nothing, want nothing.
I was certain they would see me staring through the pink darkness of my lids.
Say *get up* and *walk yourself to bed*.

Estuary

The train traces
the waterway
leaving only
a lace slip
of land busy
with broken
springs and boys
imbalanced by
5 gallon buckets
of pale belly eels
This is the end
of the world
my mother
spoke so often of
sliced to seam
allowances
heavy with
kudzu virginia
creeper moss rose
and lamb's quarters
(the famine food
the cure for boils
and snake bites)
The loose-boweled
hours empty
themselves
into the river basin
The coyotes mate
with the wolves
their heats a season
lost across the thin
lip of fen and fern
the sumac margins
the bat-lack shallows

From the express
train it is easy
to miss the shift
of seasons newly
inarticulate
to miss the curlew
the chestnut
moth the chaffseed
and milkvetch
Loss comes with
the bold rust
coated kits in
the den behind
the house the
jawbone terminus
of the migration
route to a new
latitude the river
valley broken
like a white china
cup The sound
barrier pressed
against the purring
motorway its
base shrine
of plush bears
and plastic lilies
A gilt rim
of forgiveness
for these failures
these slim
meridians
Now there is only
the lilt of the salt

of forest
The conductor
speaks the
silt soliloquy
of stations
Listing becomes
most painful
when there is
so little left

line the litany
of lichens a folk
cure for catastrophe
and passing
small station
time for releasing
the muscle
which holds
a shard in the fist

Nomenclature

I always pause for you to laugh
at the joke: how difficult

it must have been for the man
to steer his car while masturbating.

I could walk the route he followed
me down in my sleep. Liberty Street,

the snapped-down daylilies,
the horse chestnuts and coneflowers

toothing up front walks. I find comfort
in naming off the plants I pass.

Veronica. Phlox. Astilbe. Yarrow.
I find comfort in telling the story

over and over. Yesterday I showed
you the out-of-bloom violets

in your overgrown garden. Knelt
to point out the veins

of them beneath the rough growth
of goldenrod and thistle.

You pulled them up
anyway, new to the gesture and pleased

to work your fingers around the tender stem,
to tug up runs and ribbons,

to bare the plot completely.
Yesterday I tried to tell you—

the man who showed me his dick
as he pulled his gold

sedan up beside me
wasn't naming me as desirable,

himself as desiring.
He was saying simply: *I have the power*

to take the goodness
from today, from all other days.

I don't know, you say,
what violets even look like.

But I remember plucking
a spade-shaped leaf for you.

Snapping its furred stalk
so you could more closely learn

the contours I memorized
in the garden when I was a child.

Remainder

Science tells us silence
is the safest way to signal
fear. The deer flocked

at the bottom of the garden
turn all their mirrored eyes
your way. I am afraid to have children,

to shit the birthing bed, then fail
them over and over. My mother's
mother's mother got into bed

after giving birth and never got up.
Spent her days ordering silk nightgowns
through the mail, still wrapped

in creased tissue when she died.
I am afraid of something crawling
back in. A spider in the bed at night,

a hand walking over on its fingers,
dirty nails. Something
staving me from within.

My mother's mother never ate anything
but artichokes. *Negative calories*,
she would say. *You look prettier*

when you comb your hair
she would say. Her feet were teacups,
she had her little toes cut off. I am afraid

of the part of me that drowned
the daddy long legs in the shower,
turned the spray against her even

though I knew her mouth
was too small to break my skin.
That flesh my mother held

between two fingers, repeating
you will lose the baby
fat with time. Afraid of what carries

down like a prime number,
What I cannot split and swallow.
Afraid of eating or fucking

until I am full. Afraid of the other
lesson we learn from the deer,
the way a look ripples

through the herd, the way they raise
their heads down the line, mouths
suddenly gentle around the soft, soft grass.

The Husband

I would rather talk about the mirror and knot of the dune grass.
The black-footed foxes denned up under the stoop

of the candy shop all winter. The low purple music of a bruise,
of the jukebox in the bar about to shutter, the shudder of the glass

door facing the bay. The sea tearing off skin after insistent skin.
Here, at the kettle ponds, still as windfall fruit

in the tall grass. Here, before the tide-line's broken folio of stones,
blood vessels on a crushed breast. Have I had this salt-seized coin in my cheek

all this time? This wedge of lemon over my teeth, this oyster tipped back in my throat,
like the ocean spitting into my mouth, the husband into his palm

before he entered me? But I have forgotten what we ever talked about.
The secret language of years spent driving between one town and another.

I only have our joke about the pears left, and I've been trying
to repeat it ever since with no success. I would prefer to speak

about the earth's broken plates, quick as a fingernail off the coast.
Or the *s* in *persistent* meaning wind or sea or grief

or the particular variety of bravery we call desire. But I will try to explain
how I turned to him driving down Route 6 and said

listen there's something I need to ask you and then paused

as though about to confess an infidelity, an acquiescence, a crack
opening toward some secret daylight. And how, if I sold the hesitation well,

he would say *baby, what's wrong?* And I would ask him,
in the voice of an old woman, *did you get any pears?*

I cannot remember where the joke began, and I know it is not funny
now. It was not funny when he called me and let the line go wax-still

before he said he did not want me anymore, and I pretended
we were playing the game. Prepared myself to tell the husband, *yes,*

I bought you the pears. Their skins so thin my fingernails slit them into moons.

Some Oranges

*Items Wanted—(From my Note Books.)—Some of the half-erased and not over-
legible when made, memoranda of things wanted, by one patient or another, will
convey quite a fair idea. D. S. G. bed 52, wants a good book; has a sore, weak throat;
would like some horehound candy. Is from New Jersey, 28th regiment.......C. H. L.,
145th Pennsylvania, lies in bed with jaundice and erysipelas; also wounded. Stomach
easily nauseated. Bring him some oranges, also a little tart jelly.*

—*Walt Whitman,* Memoranda During the War

There are two three-legged dogs and one with four on the street
in the morning. Loss leaves my mouth with a taste for sweetness.

In the park three little girls fit their bodies neatly into the hollow space
low on the trunk of the sycamore. The roots arch their backs against the brick
blanket pooling to the playground and the asphalt basketball court
whiskery with teenage boys and weeds. This is not the sweetness
I want. Not the little girls, or the boys, who love one another
and clasp each others' jaws to shout mouth to mouth, thumbs pressed, tenderly,
by the ear, after each silken three point shot.

It is not the bird high in the sycamore who shits into the crook of my elbow,
although the shit is dense and heavy with fruit seeds. The sweetness
is not the soft place where the shit lands, the place too full of vital machinery
to quite fit into itself. It is not the coffee from the bodega,
grainy with sugar and powdered milk, or the styrofoam cup whose rim
I scallop with my teeth. It is not the three-legged dogs, three of them now,
or the one with four, who has lain in the sun and refused to walk farther.

It is not the girl I wake next to, her bunched polyester slip or her underbite.
Not the groan of the box fan or the rusty and dependable geometry
of a fire escape busy with blooms and yellow-leafed tomatoes,
too many to a terracotta pot. It is not the toothsome twist
of a printed scarf around the throat of her roommate,
a flight attendant bound for LAX, Phoenix, LAX.

Not the vibration of the telephone low against my belly,
which I slept pressed against so I would be sure to wake.
Although there is a certain pleasure in the vibration,
in all these things. Maybe it is the wedge of cake in a plastic box
I take from her fridge after the telephone call, the plastic box
fitted to the shape of the slice, the slice dripping
with fluorescent cherry jam. Maybe it is the way the girl
lifts the hem of her slip to wipe the salty wet face
of my telephone dry when I wake her to say goodbye.

Velvet Touch

No one cares about the sloppy irony of $10 dances nestled next to Corinthians
hung over the highway's tree line thick with speed. About drunk rumbles

in the teeth, the precise despair of the off ramp, the Michigan Whitetail Museum—
albino buck resting his load of antlers on the gate nearest the guard rail. No one cares

about this morning's lesson in the world's quiet violence.
I turn to release the catch-tongue on the nozzle and the man at pump 3 says

I see the deer tattooed on the back of your thigh. It's like you, wants to be hunted.
If he can make metaphors, this man drunk on always getting what he wants,

then anyone can. I made myself promise that I wouldn't write anything
someone else could or should. So I can't include this line about my new boyfriend

fishing the drowning bee from the apple pulp the day we pressed cider. Lifting it on index
tip. I've read it before and anyway his last girlfriend was a poet too, a good one, I'm told.

I can't imagine she didn't record a similar tenderness. A spider lofted between wineglass
and page. The car window cracked for a crane fly. I'll never be better

at language than the strip club down the block: *1000's of beautiful girls and 3 ugly ones.*
That perfect interval: Hopper's sunshine burning a diagonal from bedpost to wall.

There's a story I've been trying to tell for years because no one else
in it could or should or gave a shit. My husband's grandmother died.

It wasn't sudden. Dementia, but first it made her love all the foods she had ever hated.
Ketchup, honey, banana. Her soft mouth filled and emptied. Her husband was a
   biologist,

he studied redwing blackbirds. At the funeral he said *she was a biologist too,*
her greatest experiment was giving birth to and raising 3 children.

At the funeral 3 people spoke with emotion about her uncanny
ability to know what Tupperware would be filled precisely with what leftovers.

We drove her little box of ashes into the Skagit. He spread her in handfuls
in the tall grass where the snow geese were sleeping. Maybe I'm wrong,

maybe her husband is writing this poem right now and I'm in it: carsick,
my high heels sinking into the earth. How he looked around when he was done,

then wiped his palms on his thighs. *How little we are,* he said.
How little when you take the water out.

Charlotte

When I was a child the walls were filled with bees. Burr and sugar.
Seams beaded with heat. Corner of a numbed mouth.

At night doves threw themselves at the windows.
Hunters storming through the gum trees like house cats

cut from their bells, beer-drunk Gods making a scene through the ceiling.
I had a big bunny on a red leash, I think. There was a white horse

standing in the road. Asparagus ferns, yellow jackets turning up a hem.
The wormy kittens dumped behind the machine shed. The red

Corolla parked on the edge of the bank-owned bundle, swallowing
exhaust until it blew. The neighbor who

shot his wife, got off. His story—a copperhead, two fingers
on the trigger, morning glories ratcheting

up chicken wire. The honey's slow clock. I've kept it
to myself. Don't want to mourn this forest brute with history.

The shade trees root-rotted with the long blue acid of bodies.
The weight of them. Oh God, cut them down. My brother says he was hit by a car

in the intersection where they paved over those fallow 15 acres.
Built a Chick-fil-A an Applebee's, a Bank of America

and another. He says the car kissed him gently on the hip. He says we ate
roadkill. Remembers dinners of maggoty black-eyed peas. I was there.

It was C. who was hit when we were crossing from marsh
to marsh. We always talked big about sugaring

the tanks of bulldozers in the raw new lots, but chickened. Always fought
over who found that antlered skull in the lost forest. I say I lay down

in front of the mower to stop my father from cutting the grass.
I say that the start-cord snapped into its steaming sheath.

That the muscadines broke open in the mouth like the peal of a bell.
The linoleum yellow with pollen on the sleeping porch.

C. died, long after. Drowned even though he swam so well.
We were long gone, and the marshes. They plowed down

the half-slumped sharecropper's cabin in the auction-bound lot
where we would linger on the sill—ghost places set for dinner still,

forks, knives, dislocated dresser drawers, the snicker of a possum
under the range. Birth bills pushpinned to the wasp-papered wall.

They put in a Food Lion, a Steps N Motion, a Wolfman Pizza
with 15 screens on repeat. Wolfman always tearing into a blonde.

Why did I decide to write this poem today? C.'s been dead
ten years at least, and the subdivision's cum-scent rows

of Bradford pears are tall as hell. I'm ashamed to love any shape
this land has bent to. The creek oxbowing beneath the interstate loop.

The above-ground pool we filled with tadpoles, walls sloughing algae,
paw-paws and fire ants whose red mounds we drowned with boiling water.

The confederate flag the muddy hens the trash fire smell of fall. Fuck it all.
They've renamed all the places I once knew. Now Raintree, now Innisfree,

Fairway Downs, Cobblestone, Polo View, Piper Glen, Firethorne.
Engraved on sandstone gates, the toothache green of sod, 10,000 white

houses with grand two story porticos. I'm ashamed to mourn
the land once wielded like a knife. But I want to remember

the car: gentler than it's possible to say. Gentler than a nipple, or a bee.
That's imprecise.   And was it the horse, not C. who was hit?

I remember her in the road, everyone out of their cars. Arms up.
A hand on her muzzle. She was afraid and then she wasn't.

Or was the horse killed elsewhere? Ohio, Michigan, Virginia? I think so, yes.
Hit at the base of a long, sloped drive, the palomino.

Buckets of pony, what a mess. This horse is alive on the gravel road
at the end of the story. And C. was alive too, yes. Standing on the bloody road

staring into the stinking, trembling marsh.

June

Because the fridge is broken, we have no milk.

Because the night is full of stray cats, of firecrackers, of shadows of sugar locust, loosed by sirens, pressed against the door, we fumble with the keys.

Because the fridge is broken, the house smells like fruit flies hovering over a warm bowl of water.

Because the pepper spray is in my eyes, lashes, brows, and hair, my skin is not last week's skin when we jarred honey, cranking the spring-release handle to spin the frames until droplets flew and, breeze-caught, landed on my elbow's inside, which you kissed.

Because the cops threw you to the ground, your ribs purple.

Because you got up to run, hands bound, to pull the police from me, your ribs purple doubly.

Because the pepper spray is in my eyes lashes brows my face is a stranger's when I pass the mirror.

Because my eyes can't open I only know I am a stranger from of the photograph a friend took. I am at her kitchen table. I am on the phone spelling your name. Each letter is also something else. S as in O as in N as in the huge eye on one side of my face my face two faces sewn together.

Because the lawyer needs your date of birth, I am with you in August, suddenly, and you want meat to eat, and sex, and to say hello to the neighbors on the stoop with the secret glow of *it's my birthday but no one else knows it*, in your smile, and I am in the August we moved here, slept on the twin air mattress swallowing us belly to belly all the night. The box fan, the wasp nest on the lintel, the bottled water to brush our teeth.

Because we walked in the sun for hours because we said no more and would not let the cruiser pass into the thick of the crowd and someone broke the windshield someone kicked the door.

Because we have no milk you bring the bottle of vegetable oil to unbraid the tear gas and capsicum from my hair.

Because I brought my right hand to my face to shield it my right hand is red and present and angry in a way I am grateful for because it says I AM A HAND I AM A HAND A HAND I think yes, I could use this for breaking.

Because my hand is noisy I make noises too, the noises of a dog dreaming, running and biting air.

Because my body wants to continue to be, it carried me through the streets it carried me over the chained gate of the parking lot over the hedge and the day lilies in the park although I crushed them yes I crushed some lilies with my feet because I could not see but could hear the men behind me.

Because the police are murderers, we shouted, they need to be destroyed.

Because warm water is a match and I am rough paper we shiver in the shower.

Because oil is oil we slip and fall together.

Because oil is oil we drop the bottle too.

Because little envelope of keys because slip of soap stuck to the underside of the new bar, because crane fly lost in the ceiling's deep corner, because a new world, because Nina Simone said it could look like no fear.

Because we have this in common: apples eaten past the core, chicken bones stacked sucked on the plate, you scoop handfuls of oil from the shower floor and into my hair, my brows, my lashes and eyes. I hold the arches of your feet in my hands. Your chest pressed against my back. Sweet wet machine, the heart, the oil begins to tug.

The Calf

I knew the calf was stillborn
when his hoof sloughed
off in my palm. The inner cleft
like a glimpse of a woman's
thigh when my eye was yanked
to the gap at the bathroom
stall's lock. Dead inside
her a week and he had not yet begun
to rot and rip. Blouse seam split
when the wrist is held but
the shoulders turn away.
He had so many secret names.
To save her from the butcher we tied
baling twine to his hock and pulled
until our palms split
around the rope. A mouth
that wanted nothing.
I can't tell this story without
my mother in it on her knees
in the driveway.
When his hips came loose
from hers he released a stream
of piss onto our arms and faces.
There is the low noise
she makes, her head down
as the bull is pulled
from her. There are the dogs
pacing the bottom of the orchard,
the calf buried just past the fence line.
There she is, milk-ached morning and night.
There is the calf's share
blooming in my coffee,
there it is, spilling out my mouth.

Jersey Bruiser

Road-kill season
and the borrowed breath
of woodland on the verge
is the easiest exit for whatever
afterlife was promised.
Velvet & quiver.
The magnetic meridian
of interstate holds out
a handful of soft, fresh grass.

+

5 does and a fawn puddle up
the median. Loom & shuttle.
Drop of wine on a waxed tablecloth
rolling towards the heaviest bowl.
Southbound, the horizon relents,
orchard-land spindles up, trees
hooded in black plastic. They will
bloom when given permission,
when unhooked from the dark.
The morning enjambed
against a jersey barrier, the sun
presses its early thumbs
into my eyes. You say my name,
punch the steering-wheel.
The horn sounds
as though surprised.
I save you the trouble:
bring my fists down
on my sit-thick thighs.

New England

Through the picture
window the motion
sensor light casts
twinned shadows towards
the cedars, the pane.
I'm at the trestle
table paring fruit.
The knife the board the bowl
of dough swelling
like violins. In the doorway,
his admonition to the dog,
go pee go pee go pee.
The dough presses its cheek
against the damp dish rag
covering the bowl. The way
I press my face to the window
when I am hot and sick
with propane and television
and Shur-Fine cherries
from the jar.

+

At first we stick
to the lakeshore.
The hemlocks clot
the ice with shade,
blue umbilicals of sap line
between sloped maples.
Then the shore
line succumbs to
glazomania, ticking off
what's hidden behind
the dark sawtooth of treetops:

black shuttered churches, fire
stations hosting chicken
and fish dinners, fields
strewn with hog stones,
the careless intervals
of our argument cross-legged
on the warm attic floor, cumulous
pink fiberglass insulation,
heat rising each story,
the final credit of the movie
frozen on the screen.
We reach the center
of the lake, follow the fisher
cat tracks where they hunted
the cold scent.

+

A glass prism hung
from the window opens
light's envelope along
the kitchen wall.
I lie in the thin rim
of apricity. The wiry
hymen of light.
Upstairs the red
squirrels are trying
to eat out the walls.
So thirsty they sate
themselves in the toilet's
cool well. They fall
in, drown, sometimes
seven at once.
We leave their sodden
bodies on the ice moss
where they are taken
by a spring-hungry
something in the dark.

+

Sugar weather, the creek
swollen and roiled
with fish. Velvet bellied
as ribbons. He rolls
pants to knees
and pulls up handfuls
of snowmelt.

I wait to wade in, then
for the fish to
catch itself between
two stones. I lift
its thick muscle
with a shout
it spreads
its ruby eggs across
my thighs, quickening
wildly into slime.

Running

Sick on the vertigo scent of lilacs, and that animal taste a glass of water draws from the night when left on the sill.

Sick on the dick velvet of the apricot under a thumb.

On the mourning dove calls rising from the cable box outside the window.

Calls rising from her throat, her throat the color of a girl in a wet white dress.

Rising like profanity when you slam your hip into the jamb, like thoughts of laundry and death before sleep, the jangle and thump of a pop song between the ears.

The April air is a sulky mouth on your mouth.

It refuses to do the work of kissing.

Tonight, jogging home—let a hurt start.

Let it finish.

Run past the loud-mouthed old dog behind his chain link.

His young companion—so quiet of jaw and body it is certain he will bite.

Ring-Neck

I stepped twice
on the same dead dove
this morning. Beauty
opened a door, what
tethered me back?
The bus with her wide
right turn. The boys forming
a circle of salt behind
the depot. I am carrying
my dog's bag of shit, pretending
my hand is empty. The air is an animal
and also another kind of animal.
It hasn't learned a thing.
Keeps pressing on
the same windows.
Keeps pressing its cheek.

Notes

The epigraph is from Jean Valentine's "The World Inside This One" from *Break the Glass*. © 2012 by Jean Valentine. Published by Copper Canyon Press and used with permission of her literary executor, Anne Marie Macari.

Details from the story of Diane Schuler in "Autocomplete" are drawn from the HBO documentary *There's Something Wrong With Aunt Diane*.

My apologies to Jim, whose story I stole and put in someone else's mouth.

Details about ancient Persian "Scaphism" arrived via the *Hardcore History* podcast.

"Stench": National Suicide Prevention Lifeline: 800-273-8255.

"Persona" is for Sidney.

My gratitude to David, for introducing me to the film *Hellraiser*.

The title "His Master's Voice" comes from the trademark and logo for RCA Victor, based on a painting by Francis Barraud. The painting depicts Nipper, a dog Barraud inherited from his brother Mark. Nipper is listening to a recording of Mark's voice.

"Isabella Stewart Gardner": Thank you to Eugene for introducing me to the myth of the fern flower. To my family who made it out.

"June": Thank you to Amory, who picked me up and Christin who took the photograph. 1312.

"Occlusion" is for Peter.

The performance of *Antigone* mentioned in this poem was of the 2016 translation by Anne Carson. The details of the World War One battles mentioned in this poem are drawn from the *Hardcore History* podcast. This poem is for my grandmothers.

"The Husband" is for N. I am sorry—we were too young.

"Some Oranges." Epigraph from Walt Whitman's *Prose Works*. Philadelphia: David McKay, 1892. My gratitude to Anna, who read to me from Whitman's diaries at the Jalopy theater that night.

"Charlotte" is for my brother and for Cory.

Acknowledgements

My gratitude to the journals who first published poems from this collection, sometimes under a different title or in an earlier form: *32Poems, Bedfellows, Black Warrior Review, Canary, Cosmonaut's Avenue, Devil's Lake, DREGINALD, EcoTheo, Ecotone, Entropy, Fugue, Hobart, Iowa Review, Iron Horse Review, The Journal, The Massachusetts Review, Muzzle, New South, Ninth Letter, No Tokens, Permafrost, POETRY, Powderkeg, The Seattle Review, Shankpainter, Sixth Finch, Stone Canoe,* and *Sugar House Review.*

Thank you to Room Project, the Helen Zell Writers' Program, Art Farm, the Vermont Studio Center, and the Fine Arts Work Center in Provincetown. Thank you to all the women I met in those places. You made the book better, you made me braver.

Thank you to the comrades who helped me imagine the better world inside this one.

Thank you JC, for the cover and for your radical care.

Thank you to Meech. Never too much.

Thank you to my family, and to Marmie most of all. You saw me as a poet from the beginning.

Thank you to David, my beloved.

Photo: Michael Cestaro

H.R. Webster has received fellowships from the Vermont Studio Center, the Helen Zell Writers' Program, and the Fine Arts Work Center in Provincetown. Her work has appeared in the *Massachusetts Review*, *POETRY*, *The Iowa Review*, *Guernica*, *Black Warrior Review*, and *Ecotone*. www.hrwebster.com.